Title Page

Servant First! The Deacon's Mandate

Radical Humility. Radical Faith. Radical Service.

By Michael Eugene Smith

Miracles of Faith Ministry

Epigraph

"In those days when the number of disciples was increasing, the Hellenistic Jews among them complained… So the Twelve gathered all the disciples together and said, 'It would not be right for us to neglect the ministry of the word of God in order to wait on tables.'" (Acts 6:1–2, NIV)

This book was birthed out of Miracles of Faith Ministry, Chesapeake, Virginia — written for every church that longs for order, unity, and servant leadership.

Copyright Page

Printed in the United States of America.

First Edition, 2025.

For more information, visit:

📌 Facebook: [Miracles of Faith Ministry – Chesapeake, VA]

📌 YouTube: [Miracles of Faith Ministry Channel]

Table of Contents

Front Matter

- Dedication
- Acknowledgments
- Tributes & Letters
- Copyright & Permissions

Part One: My Journey

- Childhood & Family Roots
- Sicily Years
- Kicked Out of Italy & My Father's Fight
- Meeting Elder Little
- Army Years
- Final Reflection

Part Two: The Call of the Deacon

- The Foundation of the Deacon's Call (Acts 6:1–6)
- Stephen: When Service Becomes a Stand
- Philip the Evangelist
- Procorus: The Quiet Strength
- Nicanor: Faithful in the Fire
- Timon: Steadfast in Service
- Parmenas: Faithful Until the End
- Nicolas: The Cautionary Lesson
- Phoebe: A Servant of the Church

Interlude

- Revival Fire

Part Three: Living the Mandate

- Radical Humility

- Radical Faith
- Radical Service
- The Nine Tenets of a Deacon
- Modern Application of Acts 6
- The Cost of Service
- Serving Family, Church, and Community

Part Four: Tools for the Servant

- Reflection & Teaching Guides
- Deacon’s Workbook
- Logs & Forms
- Prayers for the Servant
- Ordination Charge & Vows
- Glossary of Terms

Closing

- Final Prayer of the Servant
- Stay Connected

Dedication

“If a duck can pull a truck, believe it.” – Clifton Smith

“A good name is more desirable than great riches; to be esteemed is better than silver or gold.” (Proverbs 22:1)

This book is dedicated to my father, Clifton Smith, whose wisdom shaped me long before I realized it would. His sayings were simple, but they carried the weight of scripture. He taught me that a man’s integrity is worth more than riches, that unity holds a house together, and that faith will always outlast fear.

To my mother, Shirlene Smith, who modeled prayer, discipline, and quiet strength.

To my wife, Evangelist Katrina Smith, whose love steadies me and whose faith keeps me pressing forward.

To my family, church, and community — this book is for you.

And above all, to our Lord and Savior Jesus Christ, the Servant of all, who gave us the towel-before-the-title mandate.

Written in Chesapeake, Virginia — for the world.

Acknowledgments

I honor Bishop Mark L. Thomas and Lady Naomi Thomas, leaders of the Historic Virginia First District, whose vision and covering strengthen this work.

I honor Dr. Superintendent Pastor Kelsey D. Little Sr. and Lady Joi Little, whose leadership is both rooted and fresh. Pastor Kelsey is a man of valor, approachable yet authoritative, carrying vision for the next generation. Lady Joi is a Proverbs 31 woman, leading and inspiring youth with strength and grace.

I honor the late Elder James C. Little Sr. and Evangelist Judy Little, whose faith and prayers have marked generations.

I honor my brother Superintendent Samuel and Lady Tiffany Smith, whose steadfast service inspires me daily.

And I honor Miracles of Faith Ministry in Chesapeake, Virginia, where this vision lives, breathes, and grows.

Part One: My Journey

Childhood & Family Roots

"Start children off on the way they should go, and even when they are old they will not turn from it." (Proverbs 22:6)

Every calling has roots. Mine were planted deep in family, discipline, and faith — even when I didn't know it was faith at the time.

My father, Clifton Smith, was a Navy man through and through. He believed in hard work, integrity, and saying what needed to be said in the fewest words possible. His sayings didn't always sound like scripture — but later in life, I realized that's exactly what they were.

He used to say:

"Son, a house divided against itself cannot stand."

At the time, I thought it was just one of his warnings about brothers fighting. Later, I discovered it came straight from the mouth of Jesus (Mark 3:25).

My mother, Shirlene Smith, was the quiet strength of the family. Her prayers covered us like a shield, her discipline kept us steady, and her love was consistent even when I tested the limits.

Together, they gave me a foundation that would shape the man, the servant, and eventually the deacon I would become.

Growing up in a military household meant discipline and movement. Orders came, and we followed. Duty called, and we answered. That pattern would follow me across the ocean, into Sicily, through trials, through mistakes, and eventually into the call of ministry.

These roots — discipline from my father, prayer from my mother, love from my family — became the soil God planted my calling in.

Reflection

- A calling doesn't start in the spotlight. It starts in the soil of family and foundation.
- What feels like ordinary wisdom from a parent often carries biblical weight.
- God plants seeds in childhood that don't bloom until much later.

Application for Deacons Today

- Honor Your Roots: A deacon serves best when he remembers where he came from.
- Guard Your House: Just as a father guards his family, a deacon guards the house of God.
- Carry Wisdom Forward: Simple sayings, lived out, often preach louder than sermons.

Pull Quote:

"A deacon's first pulpit is his home."

Sicily Years: Growing Up at the Crossroads of the World

"The earth is the Lord's, and everything in it, the world, and all who live in it." (Psalm 24:1)

My childhood roots were planted at home, but my teenage years were shaped in a place few could imagine — Sicily, Italy.

The Mediterranean Sea was our backyard. From our balcony we could see its endless blue stretching toward Malta. Mount Etna loomed above us, rumbling and reminding us of the raw power of creation. The air smelled like the sea mixed with pasta, olive oil, and spices drifting from open kitchens.

Growing up there was like living in a history book — but one that laughed, shouted, and fed you too much food.

Culture and Travel

We traveled through Rome, Milan, Venice, Pisa, Verona — and stood beneath monuments that had survived empires. I walked the Spanish Steps, looked up at the Sistine Chapel, and stood under Michelangelo's David. We visited Germany, Spain, France, even the running of the bulls.

It was a childhood of culture, beauty, and discovery. But it was also discipline — curfews, military order, and the awareness that we were foreigners who had to represent home well.

Humor and Chaos

Of course, not every memory was majestic.

There was The Party That Never Happened — hours of planning that ended with my father shutting it down before the first song played. There were the Stink Bombs at the Airport, where a prank almost turned into an international incident. And who could forget the night of the Balcony Jump into the Mediterranean? For a moment, I thought we'd outsmarted the world — until the shock of that cold water taught us otherwise.

Each story was reckless, funny, and sometimes embarrassing. But together, they reminded me how much God's hand was protecting us even when we weren't paying Him any mind.

Reflection

- God plants lessons in culture and chaos. Even in teenage mistakes, He was shaping me.
- Laughter can be a teacher. The mistakes I can laugh at now became anchors of wisdom later.
- Travel broadens calling. Seeing the world young gave me eyes to see people, nations, and cultures differently.

Application for Deacons Today

- Carry Perspective: A deacon must see beyond his block; the kingdom is global.
- Learn From Mistakes: Immaturity can be redeemed when lessons are received.
- Value Culture: Serving people means respecting where they come from.

Pull Quote:

"God can use even stink bombs and canceled parties to train a servant."

Kicked Out of Italy & My Father's Fight

"No weapon formed against you shall prosper, and every tongue which rises against you in judgment You shall condemn." (Isaiah 54:17)

Not every story in Sicily was laughter and sunlight. Some moments cut deep.

I was still a teenager when I found myself accused of something I didn't do. Friends had stolen money, but I was the one blamed. The system moved fast. Orders came down. And just like that, I was kicked out of Italy.

Humiliation hit like a storm. One day I was a military kid in the Mediterranean; the next, I was sent away, carrying the weight of guilt for something I hadn't done.

My Father's Fight

Back home, my father, Clifton Smith, refused to accept the verdict. He wasn't a church-going man, but he was a man of discipline, justice, and iron determination.

He went to the law library day after day. For six months straight, he studied regulations, legal precedent, and military law. He filed paperwork, wrote letters, and refused to back down.

Finally, he pushed the fight all the way to the Secretary of the Navy.

The ruling came down clear: I was to be reinstated immediately. All costs were reimbursed by the Navy. And most powerfully of all, a formal apology was issued for the injustice.

The Hug

When I stepped off the plane, my father was there. He hugged me tight and whispered:

"Son, I told you I would bring you back. I didn't let you down."

That moment branded itself into my heart. My father's fight for me was more than a legal victory. It was a picture of God's fight for us — a Father who will not let His children be destroyed by false accusations.

Reflection

- Injustice is real. Sometimes you can be blamed for what you didn't do.
- Advocacy is powerful. My father became my defender when I couldn't defend myself.
- God does the same for us. Just as my father fought in the law library, Jesus intercedes for us in the courts of heaven.

Application for Deacons Today

- Stand for Justice: A deacon cannot be silent when wrong is done.
- Defend the Weak: Part of the call is to protect those who cannot protect themselves.
- Be Persistent: Advocacy often requires persistence, patience, and faith.

Pull Quote:

"A deacon must be an advocate — in prayer, in justice, and in service."

Meeting Elder Little

"Do not despise these small beginnings, for the Lord rejoices to see the work begin." (Zechariah 4:10, NLT)

Some moments in life don't feel spiritual at first. They feel awkward, sweaty, and nerve-wracking. But later, you look back and realize God was setting the stage.

For me, one of those moments was the first time I met Elder James C. Little Sr.

Katrina's Setup

It started with Katrina. She looked me straight in the eyes and said, "Don't be scared."

That should have been my first warning.

I spent three days rehearsing what I was going to say. I ran lines in my head, in the mirror, and even whispered them before bed. When the day came, my confidence was thin but my suit was pressed.

The Handshake

The door opened, and in walked Elder Little. His presence filled the room before he spoke. My palms started sweating, but at the same time my body felt cold — nerves and respect colliding all at once.

He stretched out his hand and in a booming voice said, "Hello."

I froze for a moment, then reached out. That handshake felt like a test. A moment of truth. Would I stand? Would I shrink?

I survived the handshake — barely.

Why It Mattered

It may sound small, but that meeting was the beginning of something bigger. Elder Little would become a spiritual giant in my life. His counsel, his example, and his family would shape my journey in ways I couldn't see in that nervous moment.

God often hides great beginnings in small, sweaty handshakes.

Reflection

- Preparation matters. Even rehearsing can build confidence.
- Presence is powerful. A deacon must carry weight in the room without arrogance.
- Beginnings are seeds. What starts in nerves can grow into lifelong calling.

Application for Deacons Today

- Carry Yourself Well: Your presence may be someone else's defining moment.
- Don't Dismiss Small Moments: God works through introductions, handshakes, and conversations.
- Be Approachable: Authority should never crush; it should invite and inspire.

Pull Quote:

"Sometimes the call of God begins in a simple handshake."

Army Years

"Endure hardship with us like a good soldier of Christ Jesus." (2 Timothy 2:3)

After Sicily and the battles of my youth, the next chapter of my life would come with boots, uniforms, and orders. The Army.

The Secret Enlistment

I made the decision to enlist quietly, almost in secret. When the call came and the paperwork was signed, reality hit — and it hit fast. My family was shocked, but the die was cast. I was headed into a new world of structure, struggle, and sacrifice.

Basic training was no joke. The yelling, the running, the sweat, the push-ups — it all tested every part of me. But somewhere in the middle of it, I remembered the words of Elder Little:

"God doesn't call the perfect. He calls the willing."

Those words carried me.

Leadership Tested

As time went on, I rose in responsibility. Stripes were pinned on my chest. I became an NCO, a leader of men. It was surreal — one moment I was the kid in Sicily dodging trouble, the next I was commanding soldiers, giving orders, and responsible for lives.

The day I was promoted, I saw something I'd never seen before: my father's tears. Clifton Smith — Navy man, disciplined, strong — shed tears of pride. That moment reminded me that leadership isn't about power; it's about responsibility.

The Discharge

My time in the Army ended with an honorable medical discharge. It wasn't how I planned it, but it was God's design. The lessons I carried out of the Army would shape me forever: discipline, leadership, and the understanding that service requires sacrifice.

I came back to Virginia different. Humbled. Matured. And still in love with Katrina.

Reflection

- Discipline builds foundation. Without it, leadership collapses.
- Leadership is responsibility. Stripes mean weight, not status.
- God orders steps. Even an early discharge can be divine direction.

Application for Deacons Today

- Serve with Discipline: A deacon must be steady under pressure.
- Lead with Humility: Authority is for service, not ego.
- Accept God's Timing: Sometimes endings are just the beginning of a new call.

Pull Quote:

"Stripes don't make a leader. Service does."

Final Reflection

"And we know that in all things God works for the good of those who love him, who have been called according to his purpose." (Romans 8:28)

Looking back, it's clear that none of these stories — the childhood sayings, the chaos of Sicily, the injustice of Italy, the handshake with Elder Little, the discipline of the Army — were random. Each one was God's training ground.

I didn't always see it. At times, I thought I was just living, or messing up, or trying to survive. But God was weaving a thread through every moment.

- My father's sayings taught me the value of unity and integrity.
- Sicily gave me culture, mistakes, and lessons wrapped in laughter.
- Injustice showed me the need for advocates.
- Elder Little revealed the weight of presence and spiritual authority.
- The Army drilled discipline, leadership, and humility into my bones.

All of it pointed toward one truth: service is greater than status.

I came to see that my life was not preparing me for a title — it was preparing me for a towel. The towel of Acts 6. The towel of servant leadership.

Reflection

- God wastes nothing. Every mistake, every trial, every victory becomes training for the call.
- Servants are shaped in private long before they're seen in public.
- The journey is the training ground. What felt like random chaos was actually divine preparation.

Application for Deacons Today

- See Your Story Differently: What you've been through is part of your preparation.
- Embrace the Towel: Leadership begins with service, not spotlight.
- Trust God's Process: He turns chaos into calling.

Pull Quote:

"God trains servants with towels, not titles."

Part Two: The Call of the Deacon

The Foundation of the Deacon's Call (Acts 6:1–6)

"In those days when the number of disciples was increasing, the Hellenistic Jews among them complained against the Hebraic Jews because their widows were being overlooked in the daily distribution of food. So the Twelve gathered all the disciples together and said, 'It would not be right for us to neglect the ministry of the word of God in order to wait on tables. Brothers and sisters, choose seven men from among you who are known to be full of the Spirit and wisdom. We will turn this responsibility over to them and will give our attention to prayer and the ministry of the word.' This proposal pleased the whole group. They chose Stephen, a man full of

faith and of the Holy Spirit; also Philip, Procorus, Nicanor, Timon, Parmenas, and Nicolas from Antioch, a convert to Judaism. They presented these men to the apostles, who prayed and laid their hands on them." (Acts 6:1–6, NIV)

Teaching Point

The church was growing. Needs multiplied. Complaints rose. The apostles faced a decision:

- Neglect the Word to handle the work?
- Or appoint men to handle the work so they could stay faithful to the Word?

This is the birth of the deacon's call. Not for prestige, not for spotlight, but for order, service, and unity.

The apostles said: "It would not be right for us to neglect the ministry of the Word in order to wait on tables." That wasn't dismissal. It was delegation. They recognized that service must be organized if the Word is to be proclaimed effectively.

Story Connection: Revival Chaos

We saw the same truth in the Revival Fire. When the deacons argued, the vendors refused, and the choir canceled, the pastor's focus was stolen. But when Richard rose and the deacons moved, order was restored — and the Word went forth.

Acts 6 isn't ancient history. It's the same call today.

Reflection

- The deacon exists because needs exist.
- The deacon protects the pastor's focus on Word and prayer.
- The deacon carries responsibility so the church carries witness.

Application for Deacons Today

- See the Need: Don't wait for complaint; anticipate and prepare.
- Guard the Word: Protect the pastor's focus by carrying the weight of the work.
- Serve in Unity: The seven were chosen together, prayed over together, and served together.

Pull Quote:

"Deacons aren't chosen for a title. They're chosen to carry the table so the Word can go forth."

Stephen: When Service Becomes a Stand

"Now Stephen, a man full of God's grace and power, performed great wonders and signs among the people." (Acts 6:8, NIV)

Teaching Point

Stephen was chosen as a deacon not because he sought power, but because he was full of faith and the Holy Spirit. He began with service, but service did not keep him in the shadows. The Spirit elevated his witness. His service became his stand.

The Story of Stephen

At first, Stephen served tables. He ensured widows were fed, that no one was overlooked. But as he served, his faith overflowed. Miracles happened. People noticed.

Opposition rose quickly. The Sanhedrin accused him, dragged him into court, and demanded he stop speaking the name of Jesus. Instead of shrinking back, Stephen preached one of the most powerful sermons in Scripture — walking them through the story of Israel, showing Christ as the fulfillment.

The crowd grew furious. They gnashed their teeth. But Stephen looked up and said:

"Look, I see heaven open and the Son of Man standing at the right hand of God." (Acts 7:56)

They stoned him, but his last words echoed Christ Himself:

"Lord, do not hold this sin against them." (Acts 7:60)

Stephen died with stones at his body, but glory in his eyes.

Reflection

- Service leads to witness. A faithful servant cannot help but shine.
- Persecution reveals character. Under pressure, Stephen preached with boldness.

- Legacy matters. Saul of Tarsus was there. Stephen's stand planted seeds in the heart of the man who would become Paul.

Application for Deacons Today

- Serve Faithfully: Don't despise small duties. God elevates servants filled with the Spirit.
- Stand Boldly: Your calling may lead you into hard places — stand anyway.
- Leave a Witness: You may never know who's watching, but your faith can ignite the next leader.

Pull Quote:

"A deacon's service may start at the table, but it can end up shaking nations."

Timon: Steadfast in Service

“Therefore, my beloved brethren, be steadfast, immovable, always abounding in the work of the Lord, knowing that your labor is not in vain in the Lord.” (1 Corinthians 15:58, NKJV)

Teaching Point

Timon reminds us that the deacon’s calling is not a sprint but a marathon. Ministry requires steadiness — a refusal to quit when the work feels thankless or when opposition presses in.

The Story of Timon

Church tradition places Timon as a missionary who carried the gospel into new territories. In some accounts, he became bishop of Bostra in Syria. Others say he faced fire and martyrdom for his witness.

Whether in leadership or in trial, the constant about Timon is his steadfastness. He didn’t abandon the work, no matter how heavy it became.

Every church has seasons where momentum slows, people complain, and leaders get weary. In those moments, a deacon like Timon holds the line — reminding others by his example that faithful service is never wasted.

Reflection

- Steadfastness builds trust. People lean on those who don’t waver.
- Ministry is long-haul. True fruit takes years of faithfulness.
- Even in suffering, endurance speaks louder than words.

Application for Deacons Today

- Don’t Quit Easily: Hard seasons are part of the call. Stay steady.
- Model Consistency: Your stability encourages others to hold firm.
- Anchor in the Lord: Steadfastness flows from knowing your labor is not in vain.

Pull Quote:

“A deacon’s strength isn’t in speed — it’s in steadfastness.”

Philip the Evangelist

"Philip went down to a city in Samaria and proclaimed the Messiah there. When the crowds heard Philip and saw the signs he performed, they all paid close attention to what he said." (Acts 8:5–6, NIV)

Teaching Point

Philip began as a servant, chosen to help feed widows and restore order. But the Spirit used him far beyond logistics. Service opened the door for mission. A deacon's obedience in the house prepared him for impact outside the house.

The Story of Philip

Persecution scattered the church after Stephen's death. Many fled in fear, but Philip carried the flame. He went into Samaria — a place Jews avoided, a place marked by history, tension, and division.

Yet when Philip preached Christ there, the people listened. Miracles happened. Evil spirits shrieked as they fled. The lame were healed. And Scripture says, "there was great joy in that city." (Acts 8:8)

Later, the Spirit led Philip down a desert road, where he met an Ethiopian official riding in a chariot. Philip explained Isaiah 53, pointed him to Jesus, and baptized him on the spot. That man carried the gospel back to Africa — a ripple effect from one deacon's obedience.

Philip eventually became known not just as a servant, but as Philip the Evangelist.

Reflection

- Service creates credibility. Because Philip had served faithfully, his preaching carried weight.

- The Spirit directs servants. Philip didn't choose Samaria or the desert road — the Spirit led him.
- Joy follows obedience. Wherever Philip went, lives changed and joy overflowed.

Application for Deacons Today

- Be Ready to Go: Your call doesn't end at the church door. Carry Christ wherever He sends you.
- Serve, Then Speak: Service earns trust; then the gospel gains a hearing.
- Follow the Spirit: Be sensitive. Sometimes He sends you to a city, sometimes to a single person.

Pull Quote:

"A deacon's towel becomes an evangelist's torch."

Procorus: The Quiet Strength

"Each of you should use whatever gift you have received to serve others, as faithful stewards of God's grace in its various forms." (1 Peter 4:10, NIV)

Teaching Point

Not every deacon is called to preach like Stephen or evangelize like Philip. Some are called to serve faithfully in the background, holding the weight others overlook. Quiet strength is still strength.

The Story of Procorus

Scripture gives us little detail about Procorus, but church history tells us he became a close companion of the Apostle John and even served as bishop in Nicomedia. He wasn't the loudest voice or the most famous name, but his strength was in his faithfulness.

When others were remembered for sermons or miracles, Procorus was remembered for his steadiness. He didn't need recognition; he carried responsibility.

Every church has men like Procorus — the ones who set up chairs before service, who lock up the doors afterward, who keep the books straight, who make sure the little things are never neglected. Without them, the church doesn't function.

Reflection

- Visibility doesn't equal value. The kingdom isn't measured by applause.
- Faithfulness is fruitfulness. Quiet consistency is often the loudest witness.
- Not all strength shouts. Sometimes it just shows up, every time, on time.

Application for Deacons Today

- Be Consistent: Reliability is ministry. People need to know they can count on you.
- Embrace the Background: Don’t chase spotlight; chase faithfulness.
- Support Leadership: Just as Procorus supported John, every pastor needs quiet, loyal strength beside him.

Pull Quote:

“Not all deacons are called to be loud, but all are called to be faithful.”

Nicanor: Faithful in the Fire

"Be faithful, even to the point of death, and I will give you life as your victor's crown." (Revelation 2:10, NIV)

Teaching Point

Nicanor's story may not be told in detail, but tradition says he faced martyrdom. His legacy is a reminder that the deacon's call isn't always safe — it's a call to faithfulness, even in the fire.

The Story of Nicanor

History suggests Nicanor returned to his homeland to serve and spread the gospel. In doing so, he faced hostility and eventually gave his life for Christ.

Though not much is written about him, his testimony is this: he was faithful until the end.

Nicanor's life reminds us that the role of a deacon is not about comfort, but about commitment. When opposition rises — whether from outside the church or from within — the deacon's job is to hold the line, steady the flock, and guard the witness of Christ.

Reflection

- Faithfulness is the measure. Not fame, not recognition — but staying true to the call.
- Service has a cost. To follow Christ is to pick up a cross.
- The fire proves the faithful. It doesn't destroy them; it reveals them.

Application for Deacons Today

- Stand Under Pressure: When things heat up, don't abandon your post.
- Guard the Witness: Even in conflict, your response should point people to Christ.
- Accept the Cost: True service requires sacrifice, sometimes even reputation or life.

Pull Quote:

“A deacon’s faith isn’t proven in ease, but in fire.”

Parmenas: Faithful Until the End

“Well done, good and faithful servant! You have been faithful with a few things; I will put you in charge of many things. Come and share your master’s happiness!” (Matthew 25:23, NIV)

Teaching Point

Parmenas doesn’t get a spotlight moment in the Bible, but his legacy is summed up in one word: faithful. Sometimes the highest compliment God can give isn’t “famous,” but “faithful.”

The Story of Parmenas

Tradition says Parmenas ministered faithfully in Macedonia and was eventually martyred in Philippi. Unlike Stephen, he didn’t preach a sermon that shook history. Unlike Philip, he didn’t spark a citywide revival. Unlike Timon, he didn’t carry the gospel across nations.

But Parmenas stayed true to his post until the very end.

That’s the beauty of his story: he didn’t have to be the loudest, biggest, or brightest. He simply had to remain faithful.

Reflection

- Faithfulness is the real measure of success.
- Not every deacon will be known, but every deacon can be faithful.
- Endurance honors God more than excitement.

Application for Deacons Today

- Stay at Your Post: Even when it’s not glamorous, your station matters.
- Finish Well: Don’t just start strong — end strong.

- Remember the Reward: Heaven’s “well done” is greater than man’s applause.

Pull Quote:

“A deacon’s crown is not in being known, but in being faithful until the end.”

Nicolas: The Cautionary Lesson

"I have a few things against you: there are some among you who hold to the teaching of Balaam… Likewise, you also have those who hold to the teaching of the Nicolaitans. Repent therefore!" (Revelation 2:14–16, NIV)

Teaching Point

Nicolas reminds us that the call of a deacon comes with weight. Some traditions connect him to the group known as the Nicolaitans, rebuked in Revelation for corrupt teaching and compromise. Whether or not every detail is accurate, the lesson is this: a deacon's influence can build or it can break.

The Story of Nicolas

Chosen in Acts 6, Nicolas started strong — selected because he seemed full of wisdom and faith. But later whispers of history say his teaching drifted. He may have led some into compromise, blurring the lines between faith in Christ and the culture around them.

Whether he personally fell or his followers twisted his teaching, his name became a warning label.

Nicolas shows us that beginnings matter — but so do endings. A good start cannot cover a bad finish.

Reflection

- The call is weighty. Influence can bless or mislead.
- Guard doctrine. Deacons don't just serve tables; they guard truth.

- Finishing matters. A good start isn't enough — you must end faithful.

Application for Deacons Today

- Stay Grounded in Scripture: Don't let culture or convenience rewrite the Word.
- Walk in Integrity: What you do in private will echo in public.
- Finish Strong: Don't just be appointed — be faithful until your last breath.

Pull Quote:

"A deacon's greatest danger is not in starting wrong, but in finishing unfaithful."

Phoebe: A Servant of the Church

"I commend to you our sister Phoebe, a deacon of the church in Cenchreae. I ask you to receive her in the Lord in a way worthy of his people and to give her any help she may need from you, for she has been the benefactor of many people, including me." (Romans 16:1–2, NIV)

Teaching Point

Phoebe shows us that the call of the deacon is not limited by gender, status, or background. Paul himself trusted her enough to commend her to the Roman church — placing honor on her name and weight on her service.

The Story of Phoebe

Phoebe was a deacon (Greek: diakonos) of the church in Cenchreae, a port city near Corinth. Many scholars believe she carried Paul's letter to the Romans — one of the most important letters in all of Scripture. That meant Paul trusted her character, her witness, and her leadership.

She wasn't just a helper in the background; Paul called her a benefactor (Greek: prostatis), meaning a patron, protector, or supporter. She used her resources, influence, and faith to build up the church and advance the mission.

Phoebe stands as proof: the call of service is for all who are filled with the Spirit and faithful to the task.

Reflection

- Service has no limits. God calls both men and women into deaconship.

- Trust is earned. Paul wouldn’t have commended Phoebe if her life didn’t match her title.
- Resources are ministry. She used her influence and means to support the work.

Application for Deacons Today

- Honor Women in Service: Recognize and affirm their calling.
- Be Trustworthy: Live so that leadership can commend you without hesitation.
- Use What You Have: Whether money, skills, or connections, let your resources serve the kingdom.

Pull Quote:

“Deacons don’t just carry towels — they carry trust.”

Part Three: Living the Mandate

[PAGE BREAK]

Radical Humility

> "In your relationships with one another, have the same mindset as Christ Jesus: Who, being in very nature God, did not consider equality with God something to be used to his own advantage; rather, he made himself nothing by taking the very nature of a servant." (Philippians 2:5–7, NIV)

Teaching Point

The call of a deacon begins and ends with humility. Without it, service becomes ego. With it, service becomes worship. Radical humility means lowering yourself so Christ can be lifted high.

The Example of Christ

Jesus didn't come to earth to be served, but to serve. He washed feet. He touched lepers. He ate with outcasts. He showed us that the greatest authority flows from the greatest humility.

When the apostles argued about who was the greatest, Jesus silenced them with a towel. That's the picture of Acts 6 — men chosen not for titles but for towels.

Reflection

- Humility is strength under control.
- The towel is greater than the title.
- Authority comes when you put others first.

Application for Deacons Today

- Serve Before You're Seen: Look for unseen tasks and own them.
- Stay Teachable: A humble heart receives correction and grows.
- Cover the Pastor: Humility means protecting leadership, not competing with it.

Pull Quote:
"Radical humility is the uniform of a deacon."

Radical Faith

> "And without faith it is impossible to please God, because anyone who comes to him must believe that he exists and that he rewards those who earnestly seek him." (Hebrews 11:6, NIV)

Teaching Point

Radical faith isn't casual belief. It's confidence that God will show up in the middle of service. A deacon can't just check boxes or run logistics; he must serve believing that the Spirit will move.

Faith takes ordinary service and turns it into extraordinary ministry.

The Example of Stephen

Stephen was chosen in Acts 6 to serve tables, but Scripture says he was full of faith and the Holy Spirit. His faith spilled into miracles, preaching, and ultimately his bold stand before the Sanhedrin.

His service didn't just meet physical needs — it revealed God's power. That's what radical faith does.

Modern Connection

Faith is what allows a deacon to stand in a chaotic moment and still believe God is in control. Faith says, "God's not finished yet." Faith says, "Even if the choir cancels, the Spirit won't."

Faith is contagious. When a deacon walks in it, the whole church catches fire.

Reflection

- Faith fuels service. Without it, we burn out. With it, we burn bright.
- Faith believes in God's presence even when everything looks broken.
- Faith inspires others. One deacon's faith can ignite an entire congregation.

Application for Deacons Today

- Pray in Faith: Don't just plan — believe for God's presence.
- Lead in Faith: Step into gaps when no one else will.
- Inspire Faith: Speak words that lift hearts when discouragement tries to drag them down.

Pull Quote:

"Radical faith turns broken moments into burning altars."

Radical Service

> "The greatest among you will be your servant. For those who exalt themselves will be humbled, and those who humble themselves will be exalted." (Matthew 23:11–12, NIV)

Teaching Point

Service isn't beneath leadership — service is leadership. Radical service means meeting needs before they become complaints, carrying responsibility before anyone has to ask, and showing the love of Christ through action more than words.

A deacon is not defined by the seat he sits in but by the towel he carries.

The Example in Acts 6

The early church was exploding with growth. Complaints rose because widows were overlooked in the daily food distribution. The apostles didn't ignore it; they appointed seven Spirit-filled men to handle it.

That's service — not glamorous, not flashy, but essential. Without it, the church would have fractured. With it, the Word spread and disciples multiplied.

Modern Connection

Radical service today might look like:

- Making sure the pastor is free to focus on the Word.
- Covering security at the doors so families feel safe.

- Ensuring the sanctuary is set before anyone walks in.
- Guarding the unity of the church by solving problems before they grow.

Radical service is not about being seen — it's about making sure God is seen.

Reflection

- Service is sacred. Meeting needs is holy work.
- Service protects the mission. When deacons serve, pastors can preach.
- Service multiplies the Word. Acts 6 shows that when deacons served, the gospel spread.

Application for Deacons Today

- Anticipate Needs: Don't wait to be told; be proactive.
- Serve Joyfully: Let your attitude reflect Christ, not complaint.
- Elevate Others: Service isn't about spotlight — it's about lifting the whole body.

Pull Quote:
"Radical service is carrying the towel until it becomes a testimony."

Revival Fire

The Tension Builds

It was supposed to be the biggest night of the year — the revival everyone had prayed for, planned for, poured into. But from the moment the saints began arriving, it was clear something was off.

The air in the sanctuary was thick and hot — the air conditioners had cut out an hour before. Mothers fanned themselves with cardboard fans, sweat rolling down their faces. Babies cried. Ushers paced the aisles, whispering nervously.

Out back, a food delivery truck idled with its engine running. The vendor had raised prices at the last minute and refused to unload a single box until the difference was paid in cash. Thirty chefs and two hundred volunteers stood waiting with empty hands, ready to cook but with nothing to prepare.

Inside, the saints were restless. There weren't enough chairs. People stood in the aisles, leaned against the walls, muttering: "Why wasn't this ready?"

And as if that wasn't enough, the choir called to cancel two hours before. The musicians backed out too. The microphones crackled, squealed, then went silent. Every problem piled onto the next.

The revival was collapsing before it had even begun.

The Deacons Argue

In the side room, the deacon board was in disarray. Voices rose. Tempers flared. Hands waved.

Deacon Chris: "We can't pay that vendor another dime. The church already gave them the money!"

Deacon Eric (snapping): "So what you want me to do, Chris? Tell five hundred hungry saints to fast tonight?!"

Deacon Zack: "Don't look at me — this ain't mine to fix. Y'all dropped the ball."

Deacon Dana (throwing his hands up): "Forget the food — what about the music? The choir's gone, the band's gone. What we supposed to do, clap in rhythm and hope for the best?"

The voices overlapped, louder and louder. Nobody listened. Nobody led.

Meanwhile, in the sanctuary, the saints were baking in the heat. The ushers still had no water to hand out. The microphones cut off again. The revival was turning into embarrassment — live, in front of a packed house.

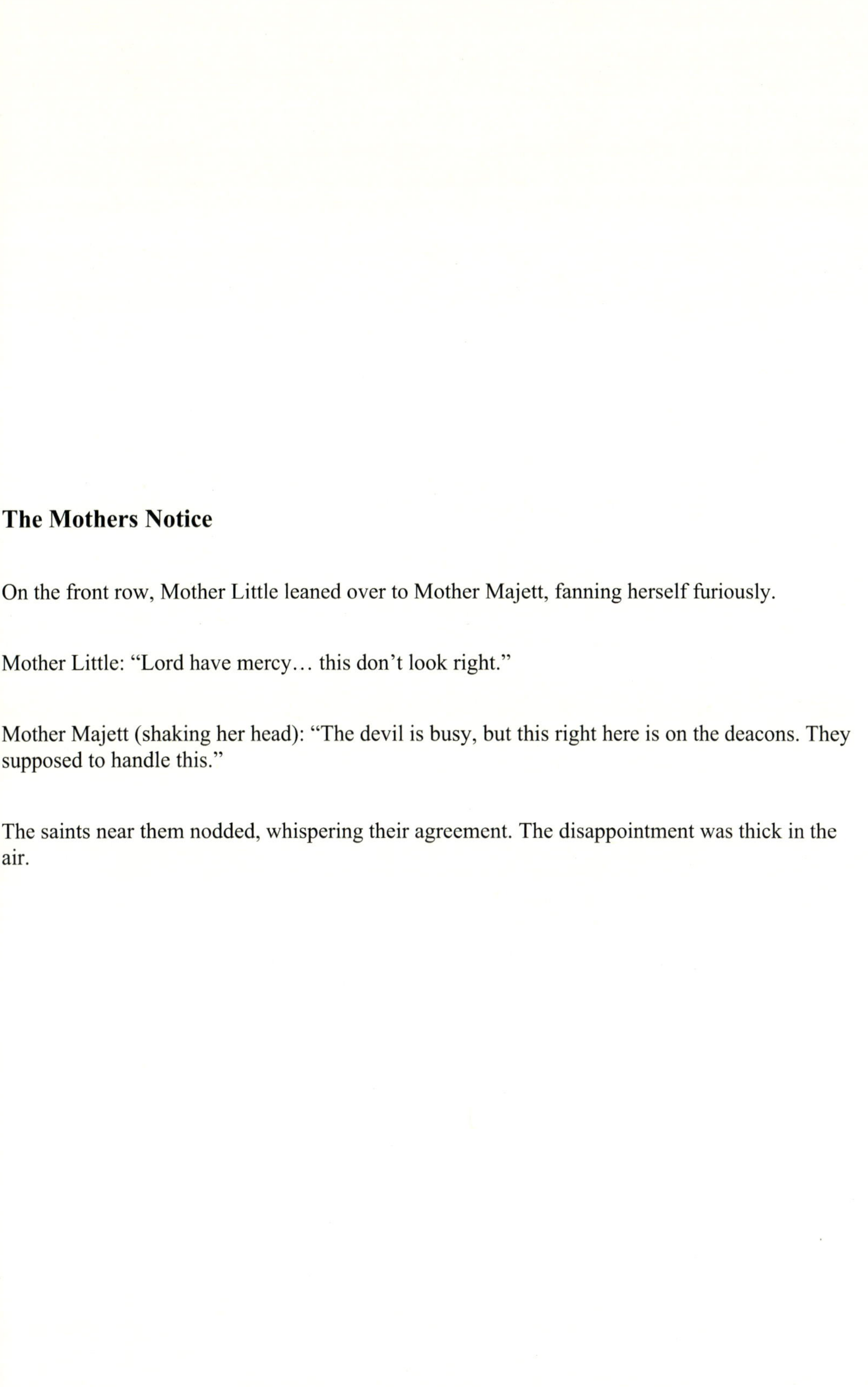

The Mothers Notice

On the front row, Mother Little leaned over to Mother Majett, fanning herself furiously.

Mother Little: “Lord have mercy… this don’t look right.”

Mother Majett (shaking her head): “The devil is busy, but this right here is on the deacons. They supposed to handle this.”

The saints near them nodded, whispering their agreement. The disappointment was thick in the air.

The Pastor Watches

In his office, Dr. Superintendent Pastor Kelsey D. Little Sr. sat with his Bible open. A TV in the corner showed the live feed. He didn't even need the sound — the images said it all: deacons flailing, ushers scrambling, saints restless, mothers frowning.

At the bottom of the screen, the headline mocked them:
"REVIVAL IN CHAOS – DEACONS IN DISARRAY."

Superintendent Little clenched his jaw. His spirit burned.

He slammed his fist on the desk so hard the Bible rattled.

Superintendent Little (angry): "Not in God's house. Not tonight."

His voice thundered through the office:
Superintendent Little: "RICHARD! MICHAEL! GET IN HERE — NOW!"

The Roasting

Richard, the chairman, entered first — shirt damp, face pale. Michael, the assistant chairman and armor-bearer, came right behind him, standing tall but tense.

Superintendent Little pointed at the screen.

Superintendent Little (furious): “LOOK at this! My deacons arguing like fools on live television. Saints hot and thirsty. Food trucks holding us hostage. And me? I find out from the news before I hear it from y’all?!”

Richard lowered his head. “…Yes, sir.”

Michael locked his jaw, silent.

Superintendent Little slammed the desk again.

Superintendent Little: “You’re supposed to LEAD. Instead, you let the devil clown us on Channel 13. Fix it — NOW.”

Richard pulled the rest of the board into the office. They shuffled in, uneasy. Dana muttered. Zack shoved his hands in his pockets. Xavier frowned. Chris wrung his hands. Robert wouldn’t look up.

The TV rolled their argument on loop. The headline screamed again:
“REVIVAL IN CHAOS – DEACONS IN DISARRAY.”

Superintendent Little tore into them:

Superintendent Little (quoting): “James 3:16 says: ‘For where envying and strife is, there is confusion and every evil work.’ And THAT’S what y’all put on display tonight! Confusion. Strife. Not Jesus. Not revival. Foolishness!”

The deacons stood in shame.

The Shift – Gabe Ministers

Then the live feed changed.

A young figure stepped to the mic — Deacon Gabe. Twenty-two years old. Baby-faced. Sharp suit. A trained actor and singer with a fire in his bones.

He cracked a grin.
Gabe: "Who said we need a choir? We ARE the choir!"

Laughter rippled across the sanctuary. The heaviness cracked.

Gabe: "Sopranos, where you at?"
"Right here!" a wave of women shouted.

Gabe: "Altos, talk to me!"
"In here!" another wave rang out.

Gabe (pointing to the men): "Men of valor — don't you dare embarrass me in front of these ladies. Where my dogs at?"

The men barked, howled, stomped until the roof shook. The whole place erupted in laughter.

Then Gabe shifted. His smile faded into holy boldness.

Gabe (serious): "I know tonight feels heavy. But God don't need a choir. God don't need a truck. God don't even need a microphone. All He needs — is your heart."

The crowd quieted, leaning in.

Gabe: "When my mama was dying of cancer, I thought I'd lose my faith. But in that hospital room, with no music, no crowd, no revival — God whispered, 'I will never leave you nor forsake you.' He carried me. And He can carry YOU tonight!"

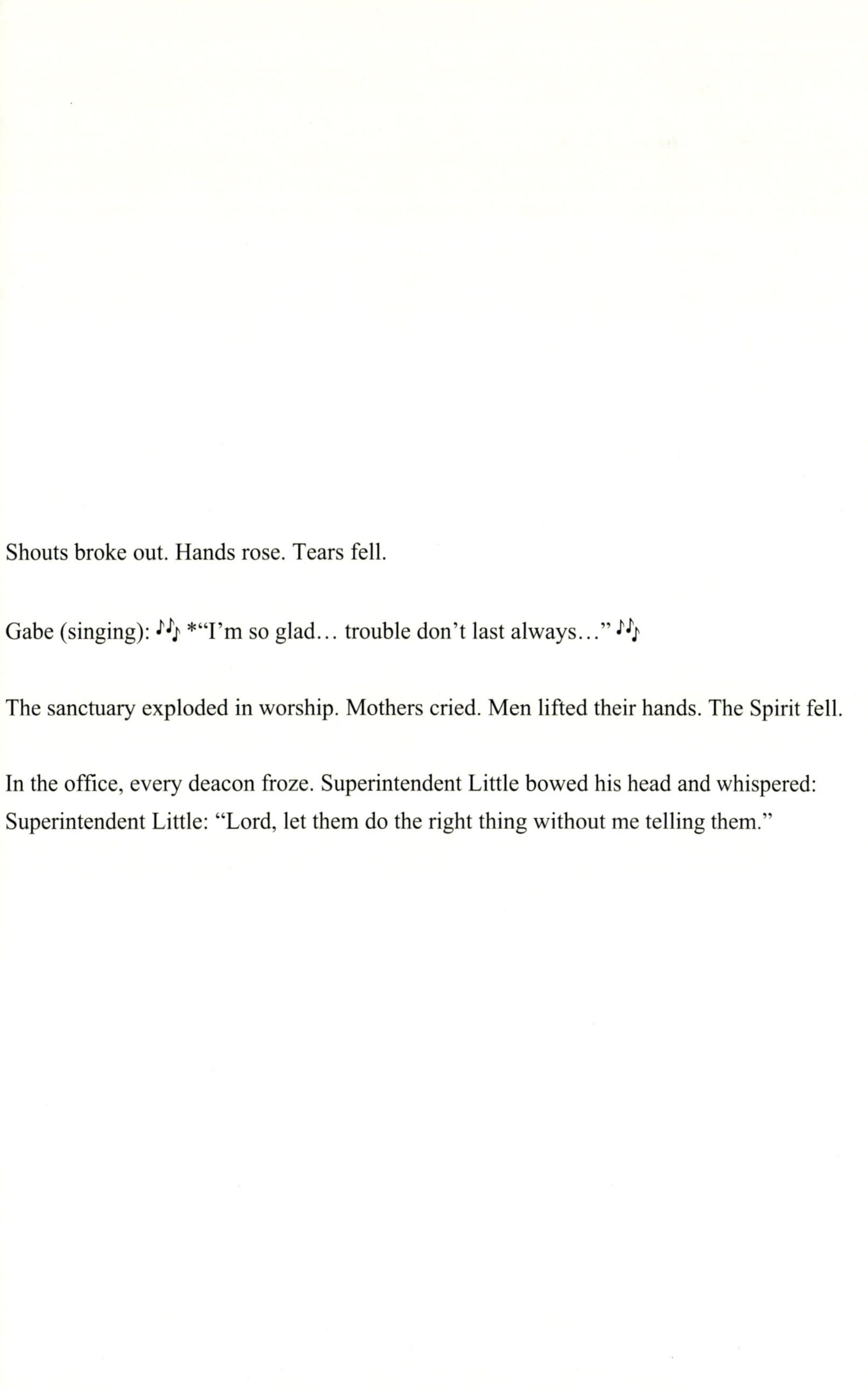

Shouts broke out. Hands rose. Tears fell.

Gabe (singing): ♪♪ *"I'm so glad… trouble don't last always…" ♪♪

The sanctuary exploded in worship. Mothers cried. Men lifted their hands. The Spirit fell.

In the office, every deacon froze. Superintendent Little bowed his head and whispered:
Superintendent Little: "Lord, let them do the right thing without me telling them."

Richard Snaps Into Leadership

Richard's eyes lit with fire. He barked like a commander.

Richard (shouting): "What are y'all waiting for? You gonna let him stand alone? MOVE!"

He fired off assignments like bullets:

Richard: "Dana — piano, NOW!"
Dana sprinted out, running to back Gabe on the keys.

Richard: "Eric, Terry — vendors. Get that food off the trucks. Push, pull, drag — but get it inside!"

Richard: "Chris, Zack — every chair in this building goes into the sanctuary. Don't let one saint stand."

Richard: "Robert — fix those mics. Duct tape them if you have to. Make it work."

Richard: "Xavier — water delivery. Find it, haul it, hand it out. Every usher, every mother gets water."

Richard: "DeShawn — air conditioning. Call whoever you need. Open vents, flip switches, fan if you must — get air moving."

Finally, he turned to Michael.

Richard (steady): "Michael — you've got the pastor. Cover him. When Superintendent walks in, he walks in guarded and untouched. Nothing touches him."

Michael's jaw tightened. One sharp nod. Assignment received.

The board scattered like soldiers. On the screen, the sanctuary shifted — saints clapping, bottled water passed, fans blowing, chairs set, Dana on piano, Gabe ministering fire.

For the first time that night, Superintendent Little smiled.

The Spirit Breaks Loose

The sanctuary was alive now. What started as restlessness had turned into praise. Water bottles were being passed hand to hand down the rows. Chairs were set up so the mothers could sit. Fans hummed as cool air began to flow again.

On the stage, Dana's hands rolled across the piano, matching Gabe's voice like they'd been rehearsing all week. Saints clapped in rhythm, tears streaming, shouts filling the air.

Gabe raised his hand, sweat on his brow, fire in his eyes.

Gabe (shouting): "The devil tried to shut this down — but God said NOT SO! This is HIS house! And where the Spirit of the Lord is, there is liberty!"

The crowd erupted, shouting, stomping, crying out.

Richard Leads the Board

In the back, Richard moved like a general. Every deacon was on assignment, and for the first time all night, they worked like one body.

Richard (barking to Zack and Chris): "Good — keep them chairs coming! Nobody stands if we can help it!"

He turned to Eric and Terry as they marched boxes of food inside.

Richard: "That's it! Set it up fast, saints gon' eat tonight!"

Xavier rushed past, arms loaded with water. DeShawn came in sweating but grinning.

DeShawn: "Air's back, boss!"

Richard clapped him on the back.

Richard: "That's what I'm talking about!"

The board that had looked lost and divided now moved like soldiers in formation.

Michael and the Pastor

At the office door, Michael stood tall, eyes scanning, headset on. He turned to Superintendent Little.

Michael (steady, respectful): “Sir, the sanctuary is ready for you. It’s time.”

Superintendent Little rose from his chair. He picked up his Bible and straightened his jacket. His face was calm now, but his eyes burned with purpose.

Michael stepped in front of him, moving like a shield. One hand hovered near the pastor’s side, the other signaling to the security detail. Saints parted as they made their way down the hall. The people saw their leader coming, covered and protected.

The Entrance

When Superintendent Little stepped into the sanctuary, the atmosphere erupted. Saints stood to their feet, clapping, shouting, waving their hands. The sound was like thunder.

Michael stayed close, scanning every angle, guarding him with unwavering focus. Deacons were at their posts: water in the aisles, ushers seated, food moving, sound holding, music rolling. For the first time that night, the church looked like a church in order.

Gabe caught sight of his pastor and smiled. With tears in his eyes, he handed the moment over.

Gabe (into the mic, voice breaking): “Saints — welcome our shepherd, Superintendent Pastor Kelsey D. Little Sr.!”

The people roared.

The Altar Call

Superintendent Little walked to the pulpit, Bible in hand. He paused, scanning the sanctuary — saints crying, deacons working, young people shouting, mothers waving their hands in thanks.

He lifted his voice.

Superintendent Little: "What the devil meant for evil, God turned for good. We came in here divided, but the Lord showed us our purpose tonight. We are not called to argue. We are not called to strife. We are called to SERVE."

He opened his Bible and thundered:

Superintendent Little: "Acts 6 says, 'Look ye out among you seven men of honest report, full of the Holy Ghost and wisdom, whom we may appoint over this business.' That's why the deacon board exists — to handle the business, so the Word of God can go forth!"

The saints shouted. The Spirit fell heavier.

Superintendent Little (lifting his hand): "If you need the Lord, the altar is open. Deacons, take your positions."

At once, the deacons spread out across the front and aisles. Saints rushed forward, some weeping, some shouting, some collapsing under the weight of glory.

Richard stood tall at the center, tears streaming, whispering: "To God be the glory."

Michael stayed posted by the pastor, covering him while watching the Spirit move across the house.

The revival that had started in chaos ended in power. Souls cried out. Chains broke. God was glorified.

And the story of that night would be told for years to come.

Reflection & Teaching: Lessons from Revival Fire

What Went Wrong

At the start of the night, the deacon board failed in three critical areas:

1. Unity – Instead of working together, they argued. James 3:16 says, "For where envying and strife is, there is confusion and every evil work." That scripture was alive in the sanctuary — strife birthed confusion.
2. Preparation – The food was late, the water was missing, the chairs weren't ready, the choir canceled, the microphones failed. A deacon is called to "be found faithful" (1 Corinthians 4:2). Faithfulness means handling the details before the saints ever walk through the door.
3. Protection – The mothers sat hot and unguarded. The saints stood restless. Security was scattered. But Acts 20:28 reminds leaders: "Take heed… to all the flock, over the which the Holy Ghost hath made you overseers, to feed the church of God." Oversight includes protection.

When the board forgot their roles, chaos filled the house.

What Went Right

But when Richard snapped into leadership, everything shifted.

- Dana ran to the piano — showing that sometimes a deacon has to step out of his comfort zone to fill the gap.
- Eric and Terry put pressure on the vendors — showing courage to confront what's wrong.
- Chris and Zack carried chairs — showing that no job is too small when serving God's people.
- Robert fixed the sound — showing that service is not always public, but always vital.
- Xavier and DeShawn handled water and air — showing compassion by meeting the physical needs of the saints.
- Michael covered the pastor — showing the sacred duty of protection.

Romans 12:4–5 says, "For as we have many members in one body, and all members have not the same office: so we, being many, are one body in Christ." Each deacon found his place, and together, the body worked.

The Chairman's Role

Richard's turnaround was key. At first, he stood frozen in shame. But when he rose up and barked orders, he walked into his calling.

A chairman deacon must:

- Keep the board in order.
- Make assignments under pressure.
- Encourage unity when others scatter.
- Protect the pastor's focus so the Word can go forth.

1 Timothy 3:13 says, "For they that have used the office of a deacon well purchase to themselves a good degree, and great boldness in the faith." Richard stepped into that boldness.

The Power of Service

That night showed the truth: deacons are the pastor's wingmen.

They are not there for titles or prestige — they are there to serve. To fix what is broken. To guard what is sacred. To prepare the house so the Spirit can flow without distraction.

Jesus Himself set the model in Mark 10:45: "For even the Son of man came not to be ministered unto, but to minister, and to give his life a ransom for many."

When the board got out of the way and got into their roles, revival broke loose.

Final Word

Deacons — don't wait for a crisis to reveal your calling. Serve faithfully before the crowd ever shows up. Stay unified, stay ready, and stay rooted in the Word.

Because on nights like this revival, the difference between chaos and breakthrough comes down to whether the deacons remember who they are.

Reflection Questions: Lessons from Revival Fire

Unity & Strife

- Read James 3:16. How did strife open the door for confusion at the revival?
- In your own words, what happens to a church when leaders argue instead of serve?
- What practical steps can you take with your fellow deacons to prevent strife from taking root?

Preparation & Readiness

- 1 Corinthians 4:2 says a steward must be found faithful. Where did the deacon board fail to be faithful in preparation?
- What's one area in your own church where better preparation could strengthen the ministry?
- How can a deacon team create systems that prevent last-minute crises?

Protection & Oversight

- Read Acts 20:28. What responsibilities of protection did the board overlook at first?
- How should a deacon team protect the mothers, the pastor, and the saints during worship?
- In modern times, what does it mean for deacons to be "overseers" in the practical sense?

Finding Your Role

- Romans 12:4–5 teaches that the body has many members, each with a purpose. How did each deacon at the revival eventually find his role?
- What happens to the whole body when one part refuses to function?
- Where do you see yourself serving most naturally — administration, security, music, care, logistics — and how can you grow stronger in that role?

Leadership Under Pressure

- 1 Timothy 3:13 speaks of deacons who serve well gaining “great boldness.” How did Richard step into boldness as chairman?
- What does a godly chairman look like under pressure?
- If you were in Richard’s shoes, what would you have done differently?

The Power of Service

- Mark 10:45 shows Jesus as the model of servant leadership. How does this scripture apply to the work of deacons today?
- In what ways can you serve behind the scenes that prepare the pastor to focus on the Word?
- How would your church look different if every deacon embraced being the "pastor's wingman"?

Personal Reflection

- Think of a time when you felt unprepared in service. What did you learn from that experience?
- Where do you personally need to grow — in faithfulness, boldness, unity, or compassion?
- After reading this story, what one change will you make in how you serve as a deacon?

Prayer for Deacons

Heavenly Father,

We thank You for the call to serve. We confess that too often we fall into strife, fear, or unpreparedness. But tonight we stand on Your Word.

Lord, make us men and women of honest report, full of the Holy Ghost and wisdom (Acts 6:3). Give us boldness like Stephen, compassion like Philip, and faithfulness like Richard found at that revival night.

Teach us to protect our pastor, to care for the flock, and to keep Your house in order. When pressure comes, let us not shrink back, but rise up with courage. Let our service bring glory to Your name, not confusion.

We declare: "As for me and my house, we will serve the Lord" (Joshua 24:15). Strengthen our hands. Guard our hearts. Use our service to build Your Kingdom.

In Jesus' name — Amen.

Radical Humility

The Story: The Chair That Stayed Empty

The church was packed for Pastor Appreciation Sunday. Saints lined the pews, ushers squeezed folks in, and the choir sang until the roof almost came off. Every leader was front and center, dressed sharp, polished shoes, heads high.

But one chair on the front row stayed empty.

The chairman had placed it there for Deacon James. Everybody knew James was faithful — always on time, always serving, always carrying himself with quiet dignity. But James wasn't in his seat.

That's because James was in the parking lot, sleeves rolled up, helping a grandmother whose car battery had died. He had dirt on his hands, sweat on his brow, but a smile on his face. He waved her on her way, then hurried back inside, sliding into the back row just as the service moved on.

Nobody saw him. Nobody clapped. No spotlight, no recognition. But when the offering time came, Pastor pointed toward the back.

Pastor (with a smile): "Some of y'all saw an empty chair, but I see a deacon who knows his calling. Humility doesn't sit on the front row — humility serves in the shadows."

The whole house fell silent. Saints turned and looked. Deacon James just lowered his head and lifted his hands in worship.

That's radical humility — choosing service over spotlight.

Reflection & Teaching

Humility isn't weakness — it's strength under control. It's the ability to step back so that Christ steps forward.

Philippians 2:3–4 says:

"Do nothing out of selfish ambition or vain conceit. Rather, in humility value others above yourselves, not looking to your own interests but each of you to the interests of the others."

At the revival, the board failed at first because pride got in the way. But when they stepped into service, God moved. Humility makes room for miracles.

A deacon who walks in humility:

- Doesn't chase the mic.
- Doesn't compete for recognition.
- Doesn't measure service by who's watching.
- Stays faithful when nobody notices.

Jesus Himself gave the model in John 13 when He washed His disciples' feet. That's radical humility: leadership on your knees.

Reflection Questions

- Why is humility hard to practice when others are watching?
- What does Philippians 2:3–4 teach about valuing others?
- How does humility protect a church from strife and pride?
- What areas of service in your church are overlooked — and how can you step into them with humility?
- Think of a recent situation: did you choose recognition or humility? What would you do differently now?

Prayer for Radical Humility

Lord Jesus,

You showed us that greatness is found in service, not status. Forgive us for the times we've wanted the spotlight more than the towel. Teach us to serve with gladness, even when nobody notices.

Clothe us with humility, just as You clothed Yourself with a towel to wash Your disciples' feet. Remind us that it's not about being seen — it's about making You known.

Make us faithful in the shadows, steady in the unseen, and joyful in every act of service. May our humility open the door for Your glory.

In Jesus' name — Amen.

Radical Faith

The Story: When the Budget Said No

The church roof had been leaking for months. Every rainstorm left buckets in the sanctuary and stains on the ceiling tiles. The board ran the numbers three times, and the math never worked. The repair would cost $50,000. The account barely had $12,000.

The deacons argued late into the night.

- Dana: "We can patch it again. Just one more time."
- Robert: "Patch? We've patched it five times. It's embarrassing now."
- Xavier: "The saints will understand. We'll raise the rest in a year."
- Michael (armor bearer, arms folded): "And let the pastor preach under buckets? Nah."

Silence fell. Finally, Richard — the chairman — stood up.

Richard: "Brothers, we've done the math, but have we done the faith? My Bible says we walk by faith, not by sight (2 Corinthians 5:7). Let's stop talking numbers and start talking faith. If God called us to serve His house, then His house will be taken care of."

The board bowed their heads. They voted to sign the contract, even though the money wasn't there. The next Sunday, Pastor announced the project to the church. Before service was over, a sister in the back row raised her hand. "Pastor, God told me to cover the first $20,000." The room erupted. By the end of the week, the full amount was covered.

The roof got fixed — not because of the money in the bank, but because of the faith in the room.

That's radical faith.

Reflection & Teaching

Radical faith is not reckless — it's rooted in obedience.

Hebrews 11:1 says: "Now faith is the substance of things hoped for, the evidence of things not seen."

Deacons must live in that balance:

- Practical enough to count the cost.
- Spiritual enough to believe God can supply.

Faith doesn't cancel planning — it completes it. The board's math was right, but their faith was missing. When Richard called them back to faith, God made provision.

Radical faith means:

- Believing God beyond the balance sheet.
- Standing still when storms hit.
- Moving forward when fear says stay put.
- Trusting that God honors obedience.

Reflection Questions

- Read 2 Corinthians 5:7. What does it mean to “walk by faith, not by sight” in practical church leadership?
- Where is your faith most often challenged: finances, people, or obedience?
- How does faith balance with wisdom in decision-making?
- What would your church look like if deacons always led with faith first?
- When was the last time you stepped out in faith, even when the numbers didn’t add up?

Prayer for Radical Faith

Heavenly Father,

Thank You for being Jehovah Jireh, our Provider. Forgive us when we lean too hard on our calculators and not enough on Your Word. Strengthen our faith to trust You when the numbers don't make sense.

Teach us to walk by faith, not fear. Let our obedience release Your provision. Just as You fed five thousand with two fish and five loaves, remind us that little becomes much when You are in it.

Give us the courage to step out, the patience to wait on You, and the boldness to believe You for the impossible.

In Jesus' name — Amen.

Radical Service

The Story: The Flooded Fellowship Hall

It was a Saturday morning, just hours before the youth conference. The fellowship hall was decorated, tables set, banners hung. But then a pipe burst in the kitchen. Water poured across the floor, soaking the tablecloths, shorting out the sound system, and threatening to cancel the whole event.

The staff panicked. The youth director cried. The maintenance team was already gone.

Deacon Terry walked in, looked at the mess, and rolled up his sleeves. He grabbed a mop in one hand and started pushing water out the back door. He called for the other deacons. Within minutes, Richard, Xavier, Dana, Robert, and Chris showed up. Some grabbed buckets, some grabbed towels, and some just used their bare hands.

By the time the saints arrived, the floor was dry, the tables were reset, and the conference kicked off on time. Nobody in the pews knew how close it came to being canceled. Nobody saw the sweat dripping or the clothes soaked through.

But heaven saw.

That's radical service — stepping in when it's not glamorous, not convenient, and not recognized.

Reflection & Teaching

Radical service means putting the towel before the title.

Jesus said in Matthew 23:11: “The greatest among you will be your servant.”

Service is not optional for a deacon — it’s the job description. The early church appointed deacons “to serve tables” (Acts 6:2). That doesn’t mean waiting tables like a restaurant — it means handling the practical needs so the Word can go forth without distraction.

Radical service looks like:

- Carrying chairs without being asked.
- Showing up early and leaving late.
- Handling what nobody else wants to touch.
- Meeting physical needs so spiritual needs can be met.

The pipe burst showed that the saints didn’t need speeches — they needed servants.

Reflection Questions

- Read Matthew 23:11. Why does Jesus connect greatness with service?
- In Acts 6, the apostles appointed deacons to handle "tables." What "tables" in your church need attention today?
- Why is it dangerous for a deacon to desire the title without the towel?
- Think of a recent event: what could have gone wrong if deacons weren't ready to serve?
- How can radical service from deacons set the atmosphere for revival?

Prayer for Radical Service

Lord Jesus,

You came not to be served, but to serve. Teach us to follow Your example with glad hearts. Forgive us for the times we've wanted recognition more than responsibility.

Give us eyes to see needs before they are spoken. Give us hands willing to work, even when no one is watching. Give us strength to carry the load and joy to do it with humility.

May our service point others to You. Let our towels be stained, our hands be dirty, and our hearts be full.

In Jesus' name — Amen.

The Nine Tenets of a Deacon

The Story: The Installation Service

The sanctuary was full, the air thick with excitement. Three new deacons were being installed. Robes pressed, Bibles in hand, families standing proud. The pastor gave the charge, the saints clapped, and the candidates looked the part.

But Mother Jenkins leaned over to Mother Majett and whispered:

"They got the robe… but do they got the roots?"

It wasn't shade — it was wisdom. A robe makes a deacon look the part. But the tenets make a deacon be the part. Without the tenets, the robe is just cloth.

That night, the pastor preached from Acts 6, charging the new deacons to live out what Paul later described in 1 Timothy 3. And as the service closed, he didn't talk about robes, titles, or chairs. He talked about character.

That's what the nine tenets are all about — character that outlasts the robe.

Reflection & Teaching

Here are the Nine Tenets of a Deacon, rooted in the Word:

1. Faithfulness – "Moreover it is required in stewards, that a man be found faithful" (1 Corinthians 4:2).
2. Humility – Serving with the towel before the title (John 13:14).
3. Compassion – Meeting both physical and spiritual needs (Acts 6:1).
4. Integrity – "Holding the mystery of the faith in a pure conscience" (1 Timothy 3:9).
5. Unity – Guarding against strife (Ephesians 4:3).
6. Courage – Standing firm under pressure (Acts 7:55–56).
7. Wisdom – Spirit-led decision making (Acts 6:3).
8. Service – Doing the unseen tasks with joy (Matthew 23:11).
9. Loyalty – Covering and protecting the pastor and the flock (Hebrews 13:17).

These are not suggestions — they are the standard.

A deacon without these tenets is like a building without a foundation. When the pressure comes, they'll crumble. But when these roots run deep, the church can stand strong through any storm.

Reflection Questions

- Why did Mother Jenkins say, "They got the robe, but do they got the roots?" What does that mean for today's church?
- Which of the nine tenets comes easiest for you — and which one challenges you most?
- How can faithfulness and humility protect a deacon board from pride?
- Why is loyalty to the pastor and the flock a biblical command, not just tradition?
- How can a deacon team hold each other accountable to these tenets?

Prayer for the Tenets of a Deacon

Lord,

We thank You for the call to serve as deacons. Root us in Your Word and anchor us in Your Spirit. Help us to walk in faithfulness, humility, compassion, integrity, unity, courage, wisdom, service, and loyalty.

Strip away pride, fear, or anything that distracts us from these tenets. Let our lives preach louder than our words. May every action reflect Christ, and may every choice strengthen the church.

We declare that we will not just wear the robe — we will carry the roots.

In Jesus' name — Amen.

Modern Application of Acts 6

The Story: The Pastor's Phone

Pastor Little sat at his desk, his phone buzzing nonstop. Calls, texts, emails — all about things that had nothing to do with preaching or prayer.

- "Pastor, the air is out in the fellowship hall."
- "Pastor, the food truck is late."
- "Pastor, the youth choir canceled."
- "Pastor, Sister Williams needs a ride to dialysis."

By the time he looked at his Bible, it was already midnight. He rubbed his eyes and whispered, "Lord, I can't do both. Either I serve tables, or I serve the Word."

The next morning, he called the deacons.

Pastor Little: "Brothers, this is Acts chapter 6 all over again. My job is the Word and prayer. Your job is to handle the tables. If you don't rise up, the church will suffer."

The room went quiet. Then Richard nodded slowly.

Richard: "Pastor, we got it. From this day forward, the tables are ours, so the pulpit can be yours."

That's the modern Acts 6 — pastors released to preach because deacons step up to serve.

Reflection & Teaching

Acts 6:2–4 says:

“It is not reason that we should leave the word of God, and serve tables. Wherefore, brethren, look ye out among you seven men of honest report, full of the Holy Ghost and wisdom, whom we may appoint over this business. But we will give ourselves continually to prayer, and to the ministry of the word.”

The early church faced a crisis of neglect. The widows weren’t being cared for because the apostles were stretched too thin. The solution wasn’t to make the apostles work harder — it was to empower new leaders.

Today, the tables look different:

- Finances
- Building maintenance
- Security
- Technology
- Food distribution
- Transportation
- Care for the elderly and sick

When deacons fail to serve the tables, pastors carry burdens they were never meant to carry. But when deacons rise up, the Word goes forth in power.

Reflection Questions

- What are the "tables" in your church today that often get neglected?
- Why is it dangerous for pastors to be pulled away from prayer and the Word?
- How can a deacon team step in to free the pastor for his primary calling?
- In what ways does Acts 6 prove that delegation is not weakness, but wisdom?
- If a new believer asked you what a deacon does, how would you explain it using Acts 6?

Lord,

Thank You for the wisdom of Your Word that never goes out of date. Thank You for the model in Acts 6 that shows us how to serve well.

Help us to see the “tables” in our generation — the overlooked needs, the behind-the-scenes work — and give us the humility to serve them faithfully.

Strengthen our pastors to focus on prayer and the Word. Strengthen us as deacons to carry the weight of service. Let the church grow, the Word spread, and the people be cared for because we obey Your design.

In Jesus’ name — Amen.

The Cost of Service

The Story: Midnight at the Hospital

The call came just as Richard laid his head down. Midnight. Sister Green's daughter had been rushed to the hospital after a car accident. Pastor was already at another hospital praying for a different family.

Richard could've ignored the phone, but he didn't. He rolled out of bed, threw on his jacket, and headed out. When he got there, Sister Green was sobbing in the waiting room. Richard didn't have answers. He didn't have magic words. He just sat next to her, held her hand, and prayed until the tears slowed.

By 3 a.m., the doctor came out with news. Her daughter would live. Sister Green cried again — this time tears of relief. She hugged Richard like he was her own son.

By the time Richard got home, the sun was coming up. He was tired. His alarm clock rang. He still went to work. Nobody in church ever knew.

That's the cost of service. It's heavy. It's quiet. And it's worth it.

Reflection & Teaching

Luke 14:27 says:

"And whosoever doth not bear his cross, and come after me, cannot be my disciple."

For deacons, service isn't convenient. It's costly.

The cost comes in many forms:

- Time — Late nights, early mornings, long hours.
- Family — Missed dinners, balancing home and church.
- Finances — Gas, food, and sometimes covering needs out of your own pocket.
- Energy — Serving when you're already drained.
- Reputation — Taking heat for decisions that protect the pastor or church.

But here's the truth: if service doesn't cost you, it's not real service.

Romans 12:1 says, "Present your bodies a living sacrifice, holy, acceptable unto God, which is your reasonable service." Reasonable service means sacrifice is not extra — it's expected.

The robe may shine, but the cost is carried in the shadows.

Reflection Questions

- Why do you think Jesus connected discipleship with bearing a cross (Luke 14:27)?
- What personal costs have you experienced in serving as a deacon?
- How can deacons balance family responsibilities with church responsibilities without neglecting either?
- Why does sacrifice make service more powerful?
- How can remembering Romans 12:1 reshape your attitude when service feels heavy?

Prayer for the Cost of Service

Lord Jesus,

You bore the ultimate cost for us on Calvary. Teach us to carry our smaller crosses with humility and faith.

Strengthen us when the nights are long and the burden feels heavy. Remind us that our labor is not in vain in You. Help us to love our families while serving Your church with balance and wisdom.

Let us never complain about the cost, but see it as an offering. May our sacrifices open doors for Your glory and show the world that true leadership is service.

In Jesus' name — Amen.

Serving Family, Church, and Community

The Story: The Empty Dinner Plate

Michael sat at the table, dinner getting cold. His wife had cooked, his kids had already eaten, and the house was quiet. He was at another late-night meeting at the church.

When he finally came home, his wife was waiting.
Wife (quiet but firm): "Baby, I love that you serve the church. But don't forget — your first ministry is here."

Those words cut deeper than any sermon. Michael realized he was giving his best energy to the church and only leftovers to his family.

So the next week, he shifted. He started praying with his wife every night. He blocked one night a week just for family dinner. He learned that serving the church didn't mean neglecting the home.

That balance didn't make him less of a deacon — it made him a better one.

Reflection & Teaching

1 Timothy 3:12 says:

“Let the deacons be the husbands of one wife, ruling their children and their own houses well.”

Before a deacon can serve the church, he must serve his family. Why? Because the church is a family of families. If you fail at home, you can’t lead at church.

- Family First – Prayer, presence, provision. A deacon’s home is his first pulpit.
- Church Second – Protecting the pastor, serving the saints, carrying the load of ministry.
- Community Third – Extending service beyond the sanctuary into the neighborhood, the streets, the workplace.

Jesus said in Acts 1:8, “Ye shall be witnesses… in Jerusalem, and in all Judaea, and in Samaria, and unto the uttermost part of the earth.” Jerusalem came first — home. Then the circles widened.

That’s the model: family, church, community.

Reflection Questions

- Why does Paul command deacons to "rule their children and houses well" (1 Timothy 3:12)?
- What are three practical ways you can strengthen your home as your first ministry?
- How does a healthy family life make a stronger deacon board?
- In what ways does service to the church prepare you to impact the community?
- How can deacons avoid the trap of giving their best to the church but neglecting their families?

Prayer for Serving Family, Church, and Community

Father,

Thank You for giving us families to love, churches to serve, and communities to reach. Help us to keep our priorities in order — home first, then church, then the world beyond.

Forgive us when we've neglected those closest to us. Teach us to love our spouses, raise our children, and guard our homes as faithfully as we guard the church.

Empower us to serve our pastors with loyalty, our churches with humility, and our communities with compassion. Let our service at home strengthen our service in the sanctuary and our witness in the streets.

In Jesus' name — Amen.

Deacon Protocols: Security, Finance, and Order

Security: Protecting the House of God

- Pastor's Covering – An armor bearer or assigned deacon should always be positioned near the pastor during service (Nehemiah 4:17–18).
- Entry Points – Armed security and trained deacons at every door, greeting saints while watching for threats.
- Offering Protection – During offering, deacons form a clear line of sight around the ushers, then secure the funds to a locked room immediately.
- Sanctuary Patrol – Deacons positioned throughout the sanctuary, able to move quickly if a disturbance occurs.
- Outside Presence – At least two deacons stationed outside: one monitoring the lot, one by the main entrance.

Scripture anchor: "Watch ye, stand fast in the faith, quit you like men, be strong" (1 Corinthians 16:13).

Finance: Stewardship With Integrity

- Counting Teams – Always two or more deacons counting funds together (no one alone).
- Documentation – Signed records for every deposit.
- Transport – Funds escorted by two deacons or security, never one.
- Confidentiality – Protect members' giving records — no gossip, no loose talk.

Scripture anchor: "Moreover it is required in stewards, that a man be found faithful" (1 Corinthians 4:2).

Conflict Resolution: Keeping Order in the House

- Immediate De-escalation – A deacon should move quickly but calmly to handle disturbances. Tone matters.
- Private Correction – Pull aside saints causing issues; never embarrass in public unless safety demands it.
- Restoring Peace – Always aim for reconciliation, not humiliation.
- Board Disputes – When deacons themselves disagree, prayer and scripture must guide resolution.

Scripture anchor: “Blessed are the peacemakers: for they shall be called the children of God” (Matthew 5:9).

Deacon Placement During Service

- Two at the front — covering pastor and pulpit.
- Two on the sides — watching entrances to sanctuary.
- Two in the back — monitoring crowd flow and ready to assist ushers.
- One near sound/media booth — technical cover, also vantage point.
- Outside detail — parking lot, perimeter, and entry point watch.

Scripture anchor: “Let all things be done decently and in order” (1 Corinthians 14:40).

Closing Charge

Deacons aren't just servers — they're protectors, stewards, and peacemakers. When positioned correctly, the pastor can preach without distraction, the saints can worship without fear, and the house of God stays in order.

Final scripture: "Obey them that have the rule over you, and submit yourselves: for they watch for your souls" (Hebrews 13:17).

Deacon Protocol Manual

---

1. Security & Protection Protocols

- Pastor's Covering – One deacon (armor bearer) assigned to pastor at all times.
- Entry Points – Armed/trained deacons at doors, greeting while watching.
- Sanctuary Presence – Two at the front, two in the middle, two in the back, plus one near sound booth.
- Perimeter – At least one outside monitoring parking lot and flow.
- Emergency Response – Know exits, rally points, first aid, and communication chain.

Scripture: "Watch ye, stand fast in the faith, quit you like men, be strong" (1 Corinthians 16:13).

2. Offering & Finance Protocols

- Collection – Deacons form protective line around ushers.
- Transport – Offering carried to secure room immediately.
- Counting – Always two or more deacons together; never one alone.
- Documentation – Written/signed record after each count.
- Deposit – Funds escorted by two people, locked bag, direct to bank drop.

Scripture: “It is required in stewards, that a man be found faithful” (1 Corinthians 4:2).

3. Altar Call Protocols

- Positions – Deacons form a half-circle at altar edges to cover flow.
- Assistants – Catchers behind saints being prayed for.
- Ministry Flow – Deacons watch for order, keep tissues/cloths ready, cover modesty.
- Protection – Guard the pastor during laying on of hands.
- Follow-up – Deacons gather names of new converts for discipleship team.

Scripture: "Let all things be done decently and in order" (1 Corinthians 14:40).

4. Communion Protocols

- Preparation – Deacons set table, prepare bread and juice with reverence.
- Sanctity – Handle elements with prayer and respect.
- Distribution – Organized, quiet, orderly. Deacons assist pastors/elders.
- Cleanup – Reverent disposal, nothing wasted or mishandled.

Scripture: “This do in remembrance of me” (Luke 22:19).

5. Baptism Protocols

- Preparation – Towels, robes, water temperature checked.
- Safety – Deacons help candidates in/out of water, prevent slips.
- Privacy – Cover candidates respectfully.
- Follow-up – Escort to changing area, provide support.

Scripture: "Repent, and be baptized every one of you" (Acts 2:38).

6. Conflict Resolution Protocols

- Immediate Response – Deacons move calmly to de-escalate.
- Tone – Firm but respectful, no shouting unless safety demands it.
- Private Correction – Pull aside, never embarrass unless public safety at risk.
- Reconciliation – End goal is peace, not punishment.
- Board Conflicts – Handled in prayer, with scripture as final authority.

Scripture: “Blessed are the peacemakers” (Matthew 5:9).

7. Emergency Protocols

- Medical – First aid kit location, CPR-trained deacons, 911 call chain.
- Fire – Deacons at exits guiding saints out calmly.
- Power Outage – Flashlights on hand, order maintained.
- Threats – Immediate communication to pastor/security captain, deacons cover exits.

Scripture: “Be sober, be vigilant” (1 Peter 5:8).

9. Community Outreach Protocols

- Food & Clothing Drives – Deacons lead logistics, distribution.
- Neighborhood Watch – Partner with community to keep streets safe.
- School & Youth Support – Tutoring, mentoring, presence at events.

Scripture: "Ye are the light of the world. A city that is set on a hill cannot be hid" (Matthew 5:14).

Part Four: Tools for the Servant

---

1. Reflection & Teaching Guides

For every chapter (Radical Humility, Radical Faith, etc.), we give discussion starters + group exercises.

Example:

- Radical Humility → "List three tasks in the church nobody wants to do. Now pick one and commit to it this week."
- Radical Faith → "Look at your church budget. Where could faith take the place of fear?"

Scripture Anchor: James 1:22 — "Be ye doers of the word, and not hearers only."

2. The Deacon's Workbook

This is where boards get practical assignments.

- Case Study: "The choir cancels last minute, and the sound system fails. How would your board handle it?"
- Role Play: Act out a conflict between two saints over seating. Deacons must resolve it in 5 minutes with scripture.
- Personal Assignment: Write a one-page reflection on what "the towel before the title" means to you.

Scripture Anchor: Proverbs 27:17 — "Iron sharpeneth iron; so a man sharpeneth the countenance of his friend."

3. Logs & Forms

Deacons need accountability. This section includes templates:

- Family Devotion Log → tracking prayer & scripture time at home.
- Service Log → list tasks completed weekly (security, offering, visits).
- Community Outreach Log → who was visited, helped, or mentored.
- Incident Report → when disturbances or emergencies occur, so boards can review.

Scripture Anchor: Habakkuk 2:2 — “Write the vision, and make it plain.”

4. Prayers for the Servant

Short, powerful prayers deacons can use before meetings or services. Examples:

- Prayer for Unity: “Lord, keep us from strife, bind us in one accord.”
- Prayer for Wisdom: “Holy Ghost, guide every decision we make.”
- Prayer for Courage: “Strengthen us to stand watch in the sanctuary.”
- Prayer for Service: “Let our hands be dirty, but our hearts be clean.”

Scripture Anchor: 1 Thessalonians 5:17 — “Pray without ceasing.”

5. Ordination Charge & Vows

A full ceremony script:

- Charge: Pastor challenges candidates with Acts 6 and 1 Timothy 3.
- Vows: Deacons pledge loyalty to Christ, their pastor, and their church.
- Presentation: Pastor lays hands, congregation affirms, board welcomes them.
- Closing: “Well done, thou good and faithful servant” (Matthew 25:21).

This makes the book usable for bishops during actual installations.

6. Glossary of Terms

Plain, sharp definitions:

- Armor Bearer → Deacon assigned to protect and assist the pastor.
- Serving Tables → Handling practical needs so Word and prayer can flow.
- Chairman → Deacon who leads board with order, boldness, and humility.
- Unity → Walking as one to keep confusion out of the sanctuary.

Scripture Anchor: Psalm 119:130 — "The entrance of thy words giveth light; it giveth understanding unto the simple."

Reflection & Teaching Guides

Guide for Radical Humility

Discussion Questions

1. Why do leaders struggle with recognition versus humility?
2. How does Philippians 2:3–4 challenge our natural instincts?
3. Where in your church could hidden service make the biggest difference?

Exercise

- Each deacon commits to do one unseen task this week (set up chairs, clean bathrooms, mop floors). Report back at next meeting.

Scripture Anchor: "Do nothing out of selfish ambition… rather, in humility value others above yourselves." (Philippians 2:3)

Guide for Radical Faith

Discussion Questions

1. When have you seen God provide after faith was exercised?
2. How do you balance "counting the cost" with "trusting God"?
3. Why is faith critical for deacons handling church finances?

Exercise

- Review your church's biggest current challenge. Write down how you would solve it by sight (logic) and by faith (trusting God). Compare.

Scripture Anchor: "For we walk by faith, not by sight." (2 Corinthians 5:7)

Guide for Radical Service

Discussion Questions

1. Why does Jesus connect greatness with serving (Matt 23:11)?
2. What tasks in your church are most often ignored?
3. How does "towel before title" look in real life?

Exercise

- In pairs, role-play a scenario where a major issue happens (spill, late vendor, broken mic). Practice responding as deacons with humility and order.

Scripture Anchor: "The greatest among you will be your servant." (Matthew 23:11)

Guide for The Nine Tenets of a Deacon

Discussion Questions

1. Which tenet do you live out most naturally? Which one challenges you?
2. Why does loyalty to the pastor protect the church?
3. How does unity among deacons affect the whole congregation?

Exercise

- Each deacon chooses one tenet to focus on for 30 days. Track progress in a journal and report back.

Scripture Anchor: “Holding the mystery of the faith in a pure conscience.” (1 Timothy 3:9)

Guide for Modern Application of Acts 6

Discussion Questions

1. What are the “tables” in today’s church?
2. Why is it dangerous for pastors to be pulled from Word and prayer?
3. How can deacons lighten the load for leaders?

Exercise

- Make a list of overlooked “tables” in your church (transportation, security, widows, etc.). Assign a deacon to each table.

Scripture Anchor: “But we will give ourselves continually to prayer, and to the ministry of the word.” (Acts 6:4)

Guide for The Cost of Service

Discussion Questions

1. Why must service cost something?
2. How does Romans 12:1 define "reasonable service"?
3. How can deacons avoid burnout when the cost feels heavy?

Exercise

- Each deacon writes down one sacrifice they've made for ministry. Share testimonies in the next board meeting.

Scripture Anchor: "Present your bodies a living sacrifice…" (Romans 12:1)

Guide for Serving Family, Church, and Community

Discussion Questions

1. Why is family the first pulpit (1 Timothy 3:12)?
2. How does a strong home strengthen church leadership?
3. What are ways deacons can carry service into their community?

Exercise

- Deacons schedule a family devotion night, then report how it impacted their home. Plan a board-led community service project.

Scripture Anchor: "But as for me and my house, we will serve the Lord." (Joshua 24:15)

The Deacon's Workbook: Case Studies

Case Study 1: The Choir Cancels

It's Friday night revival. Fifteen minutes before service starts, the youth choir director walks in with tears in her eyes. "Pastor, none of the kids showed up tonight. We have no choir." The pastor looks at the deacons. The sanctuary is full, the saints are waiting, and the music department is silent.

Discussion:

- How should the deacons respond immediately?
- What role does humility play in stepping into the gap?
- Who takes leadership, and how does unity matter here?

Scripture Anchor: "Behold, how good and how pleasant it is for brethren to dwell together in unity." (Psalm 133:1)

Case Study 2: The Offering Disruption

During Sunday morning offering, a visitor stands up in the middle of the aisle, shouting about how the church spends its money. Ushers freeze, the saints whisper, and tension fills the air. The pastor looks to the deacons.

Discussion:

- How do the deacons keep order without embarrassing the visitor?
- How should finance protocols (protection, transport, integrity) be followed under pressure?
- How do peacemakers keep the Spirit flowing?

Scripture Anchor: "Let all things be done decently and in order." (1 Corinthians 14:40)

Case Study 3: The Sick Saint

During high praise, Sister Johnson faints in the second row. The musicians stop, people scream, and the service comes to a halt. Some run toward her, others panic.

Discussion:

- Which deacon checks on her immediately?
- Who clears space and signals for a nurse or 911?
- How do the other deacons maintain calm so the Spirit of worship doesn’t turn to chaos?

Scripture Anchor: “Be sober, be vigilant.” (1 Peter 5:8)

Case Study 4: The Parking Lot Argument

Two brothers get into a shouting match in the parking lot after Bible study. It starts over a parking spot, but it escalates to threats. Saints begin gathering around, watching.

Discussion:

- Who steps in first, and how?
- How does conflict resolution (private, respectful, scripture-centered) apply here?
- How do deacons protect the witness of the church in front of the community?

Scripture Anchor: "Blessed are the peacemakers: for they shall be called the children of God." (Matthew 5:9)

Case Study 5: The Pastor's Distraction

Pastor is in his study preparing for the Word. A constant stream of saints keeps knocking: "Pastor, the toilet's clogged." "Pastor, we're out of paper towels." "Pastor, the livestream isn't working." He can't focus, and by service time, he's drained.

Discussion:

- What did the deacons fail to do here?
- How does Acts 6 show the difference between pastor's role and deacons' role?
- What protocols should be in place to keep this from happening again?

Scripture Anchor: "But we will give ourselves continually to prayer, and to the ministry of the word." (Acts 6:4)

The Deacon's Workbook: Personal Assignments

1. Radical Humility Challenge

Spend one week doing unseen tasks at church (set up chairs, clean bathrooms, mop floors). Write a reflection: What did I learn about myself when nobody saw me serving?

2. Radical Faith Journal

Think of one area in your church that seems impossible (finances, outreach, staffing). Journal how God could move if faith was applied first.

3. Radical Service Check-In

List 3 ways you served this month. Were they convenient or costly? Circle the one that stretched you most.

4. Family First Exercise

Plan and lead one devotion with your family. Write down how it impacted your home.

Scripture Anchor: "Examine yourselves, whether ye be in the faith; prove your own selves." (2 Corinthians 13:5)

Logs & Forms

Family Devotion Log

Date | Scripture | Who Participated | Reflection

Service Log

Date | Task | Hours Served | Witnessed Outcome

Community Outreach Log

Date | Activity | People Served | Notes

Incident Report Form

Date | Event | What Happened | Deacons Involved | Resolution

Scripture Anchor: “Write the vision, and make it plain.” (Habakkuk 2:2)

Prayers for the Servant

- Prayer for Unity:

  "Lord, keep us from strife, bind us in one accord, and let peace rule in every decision."
- Prayer for Wisdom:

  "Holy Ghost, guide every word and plan. Let us not lean on our own understanding."
- Prayer for Courage:

  "Strengthen us to stand watch in the sanctuary. Make us bold but not reckless."
- Prayer for Service:

  "Let our hands get dirty, our feet get tired, but our hearts stay pure."

Scripture Anchor: "Pray without ceasing." (1 Thessalonians 5:17)

Ordination Charge & Vows

Charge (Pastor):

"Do you accept the call of Acts 6, to serve tables, guard the flock, and protect the ministry of the Word?"

Response (Candidates):

"We do, by God's grace."

Vows:

- I vow to walk in faithfulness, humility, and integrity.
- I vow to serve my pastor and church with loyalty and courage.
- I vow to guard the house of God with vigilance and prayer.

Closing (Pastor):

"Well done, thou good and faithful servant." (Matthew 25:21)

Glossary of Terms

- Armor Bearer → Deacon assigned to guard and assist the pastor.
- Serving Tables → Handling practical needs so prayer and the Word can flow.
- Chairman → Deacon who leads the board with order, boldness, and humility.
- Unity → Walking as one, keeping confusion out of the house.
- Stewardship → Faithful management of time, money, and responsibility.
- Wingman → The deacon's role: supporting and covering the pastor.

Scripture Anchor: "The entrance of thy words giveth light." (Psalm 119:130)

Final Charge: Servant First!

The journey of the deacon is not about titles, chairs, or boards. It is about towels, tables, and service. Acts 6 reminds us that when deacons walk in unity, the Word of God spreads, and the church multiplies.

We have laughed, cried, reflected, and even walked through revival together in these pages. But the work does not stop here. Every assignment, every case study, every late-night call to pray over a family — all of it builds the testimony of a servant.

So I leave you with this charge:

Deacons, be the pastor's wingman. Be the saints' protector. Be the church's example.

When you walk in Radical Humility, Radical Faith, and Radical Service, you carry the very heartbeat of Christ into the sanctuary and into the streets.

And when it feels heavy, remember the words of Jesus:

"Well done, thou good and faithful servant… enter thou into the joy of thy lord." (Matthew 25:21)

Closing Prayer

"Lord, make us faithful.
Keep our hands steady, our eyes watchful, and our hearts pure.
Let us serve with joy, protect with courage, and love without limit.
And when our work on this side is done,
may we be found worthy to hear You say,
'Servant first, well done.'

In Jesus' name, Amen."

About the Author

Michael Eugene Smith is a servant first — a husband, father, veteran, and deacon whose life has been shaped by family, faith, and service. Born into a U.S. Navy household and raised overseas, Michael's journey has taken him from the discipline of military life to the front lines of ministry in the Black church.

He is a proud member and deacon under the leadership of Dr. Superintendent Pastor Kelsey D. Little Sr. and Lady Joi Little at Miracles of Faith Ministry, Chesapeake, Virginia. Guided by the wisdom of Bishop Mark Anthony Thomas and Lady Naomi Thomas of the Historic Virginia First Ecclesiastical Jurisdiction, Michael's ministry is rooted in order, humility, and revival fire.

With a voice that blends humor, authenticity, and scripture, Michael has become known as a storyteller who makes the Word real. His passion is training deacons and leaders to understand their calling: to protect, to serve, and to carry the weight of the church with integrity.

Through his writing, he continues the mandate of Acts 6 — equipping a new generation of deacons with the tools, courage, and radical faith needed to serve the church in power.

📖 Servant First! The Deacon's Mandate is his debut manual, written to inspire boards, encourage pastors, and remind the church that true greatness begins with a towel.

Connect with Miracles of Faith Ministry:

🖥 YouTube: Miracles of Faith Ministry

📘 Facebook: Miracles of Faith Ministry – Chesapeake, Virginia

.

Made in United States
North Haven, CT
25 September 2025